SUMMER
LEARNING WORKBOOK

Cindy Broky

Table of Contents

Introduction

For children having trouble with their studies (or for those who are very advanced), school can be painful for both kids and their parents. It can be frustrating and can leave kids dreading school - something parents want to avoid any way they can. So, what's a parent to do?

The solution is to get a workbook that has a fun, highly-interactive handheld learning system. A summer learning workbook is the one and only system of its kind.

Much different from video games and even other educational electronics, the summer learning workbook provides a completely customizable learning experience that is self-paced and automatically adjusts to a child's abilities and skill levels to challenge them without overwhelming them.

The best part is that as the child is busy revising this book with all their favorite images and pictures, they're learning new skills in reading, language, math and science (or brushing up on what they've already learned).

For kids with short attention spans who grow bored q uickly (pretty much all of them!), a summer learning workbook is a great way to keep the fun going without a run to the store for new games. Parents will love the convenience and kids will love the variety, challenge and positive feedback for a job well done via the workbook.

At home and on the go, kids will find the workbook a great way to learn new concepts while strengthening skills learned in school.

Parents who choose to buy workbooks give their kids an academic boost if they're having a tough time in school will also get the peace of mind of knowing their kids are learning from a company dedicated to their needs.

This summer learning workbook is written by an author who understands the importance of making the educational experience a fun one for children so that they'll stick with it and learn more and retain their skills longer.

So, whether school's out for summer, your child needs more study time, or your advanced child needs more challenging lessons, this summer learning workbook will help you create the most customizable learning guide for your kids.

Thanks for downloading this book!

Exercise - a

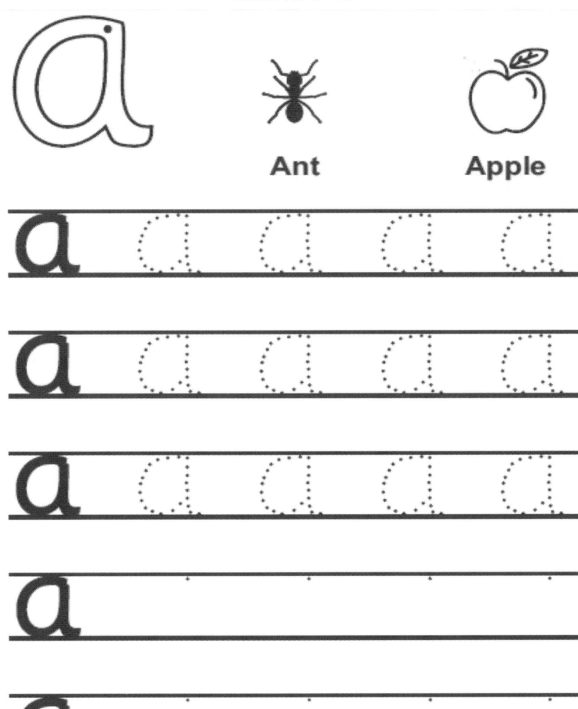

Ant   **Apple**

Exercise - b

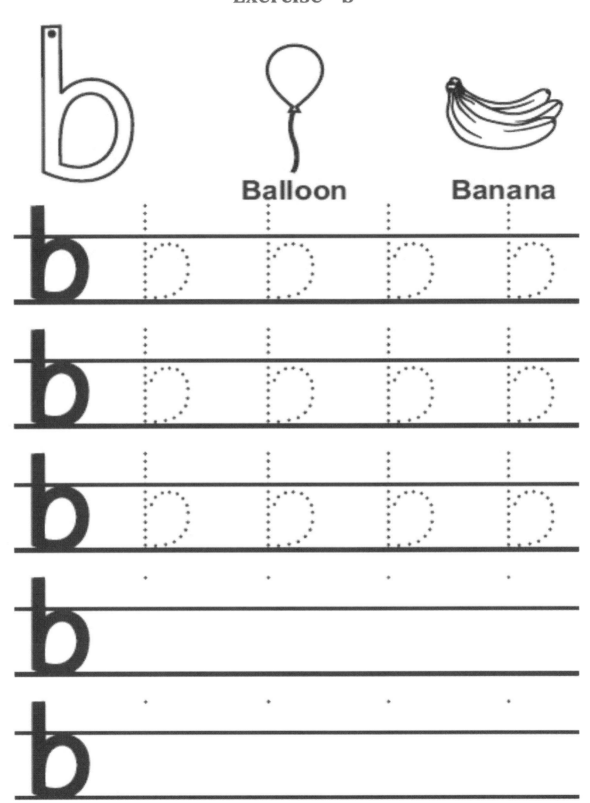

Balloon   Banana

Exercise – c

Cat

Cake

 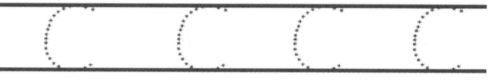

 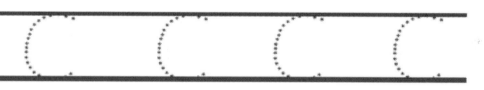

 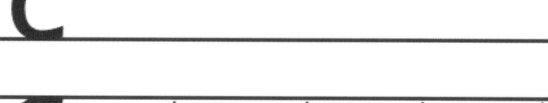

Exercise - d

Dog

Doll

Exercise - e

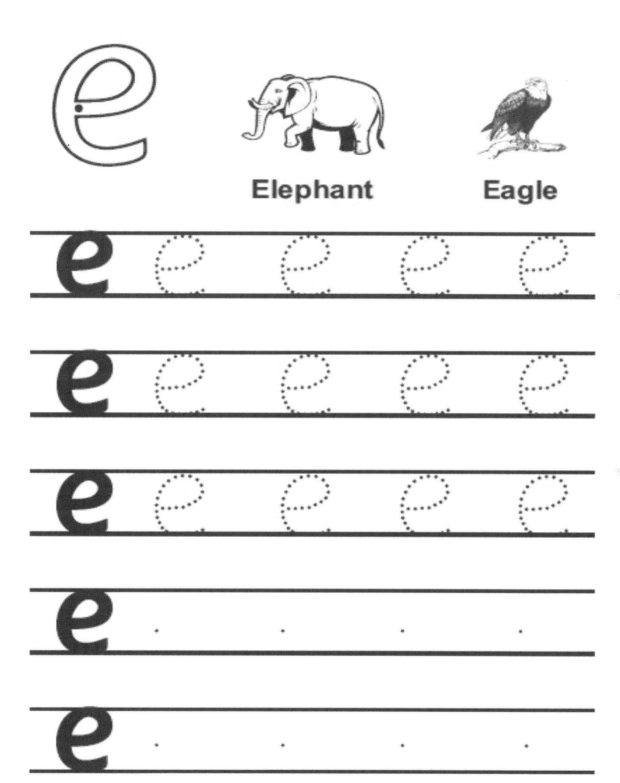

Elephant　　　　**Eagle**

Exercise - f

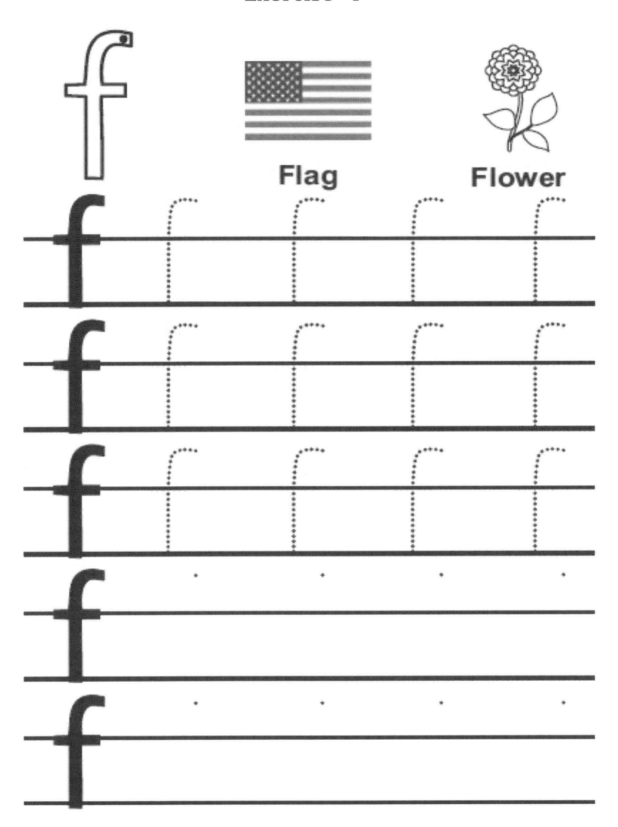

Flag

Flower

Exercise - g

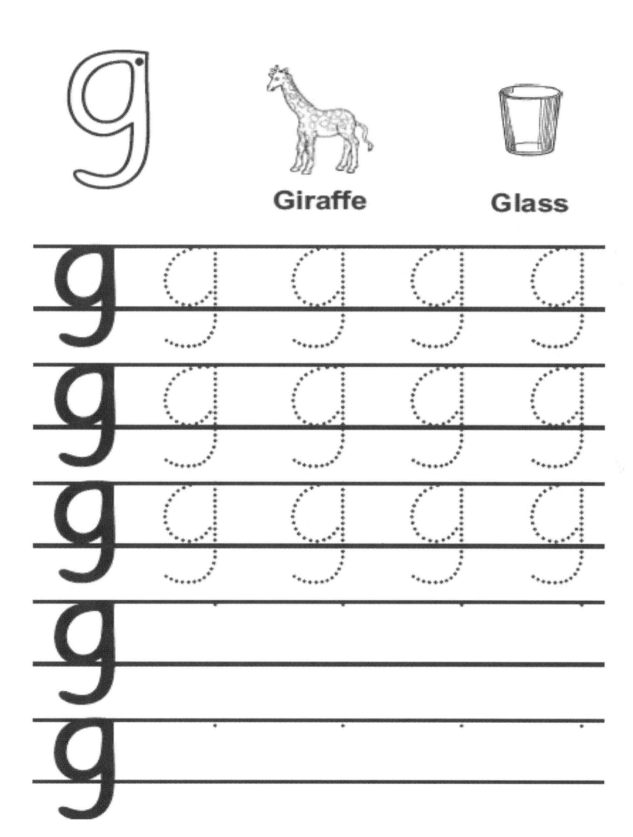

Giraffe   Glass

Exercise - h

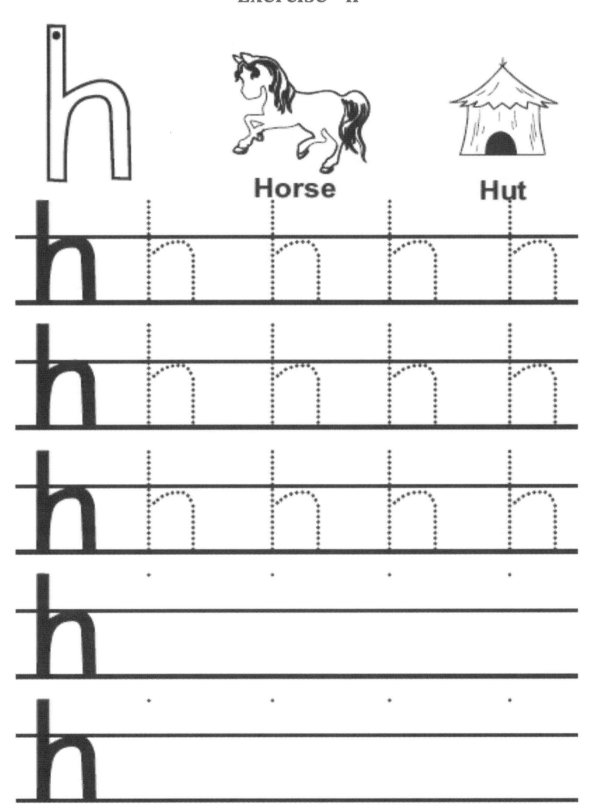

Horse

Hut

Exercise - i

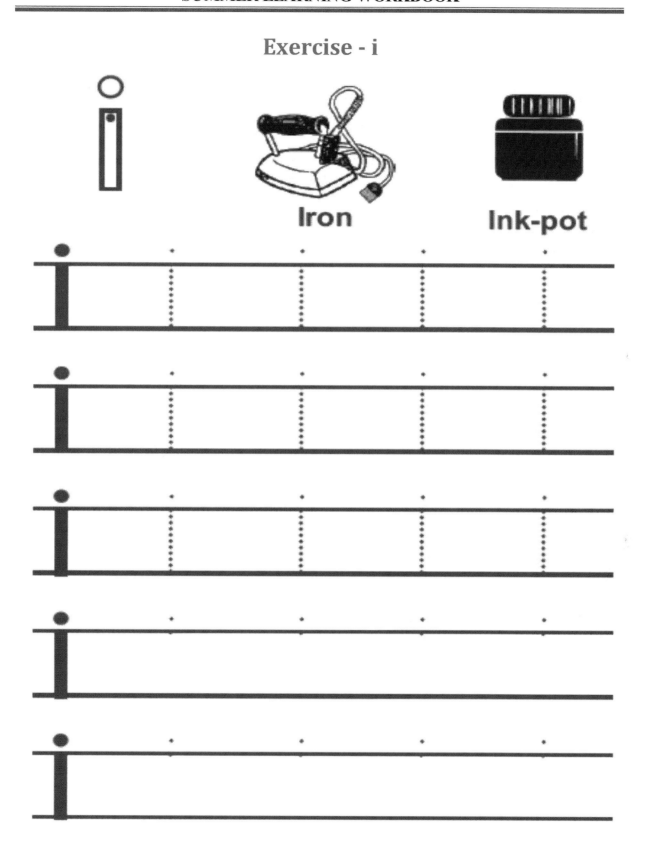

Iron   Ink-pot

Exercise - j

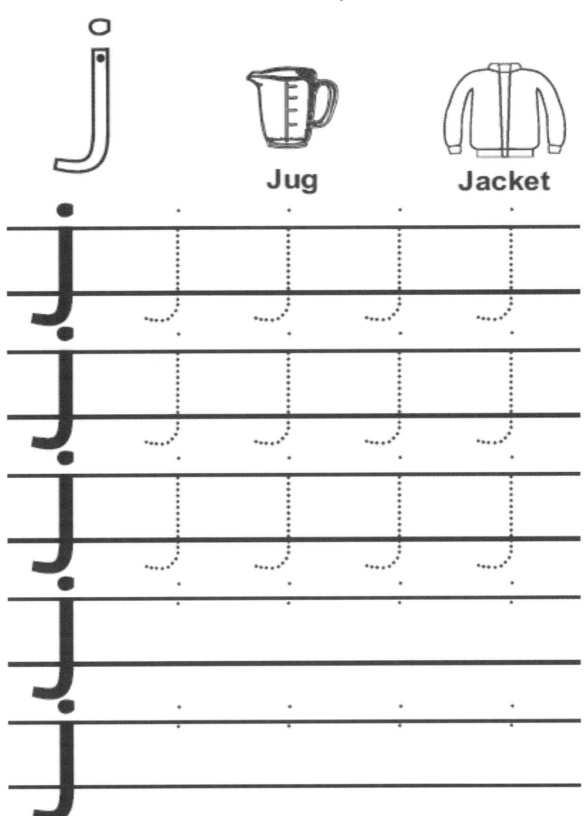

Jug

Jacket

Exercise - k

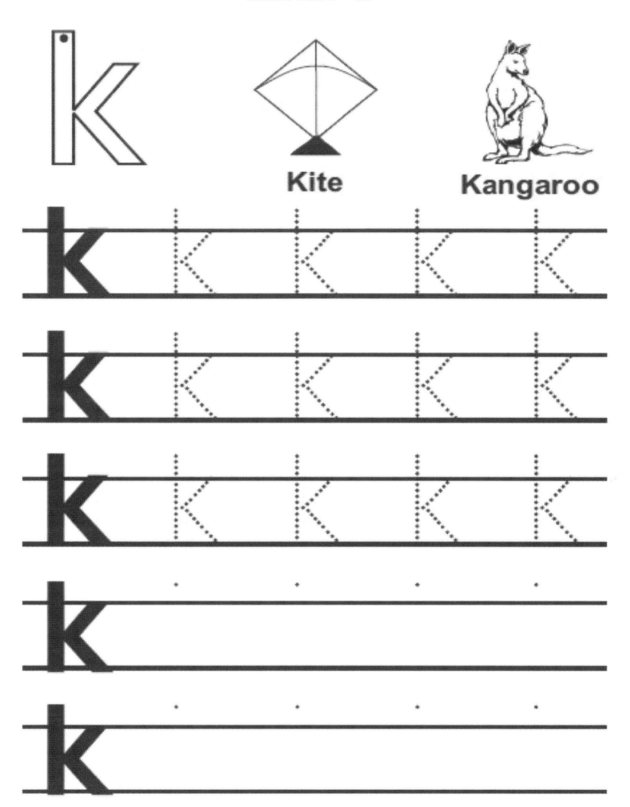

Kite   **Kangaroo**

Exercise - 1

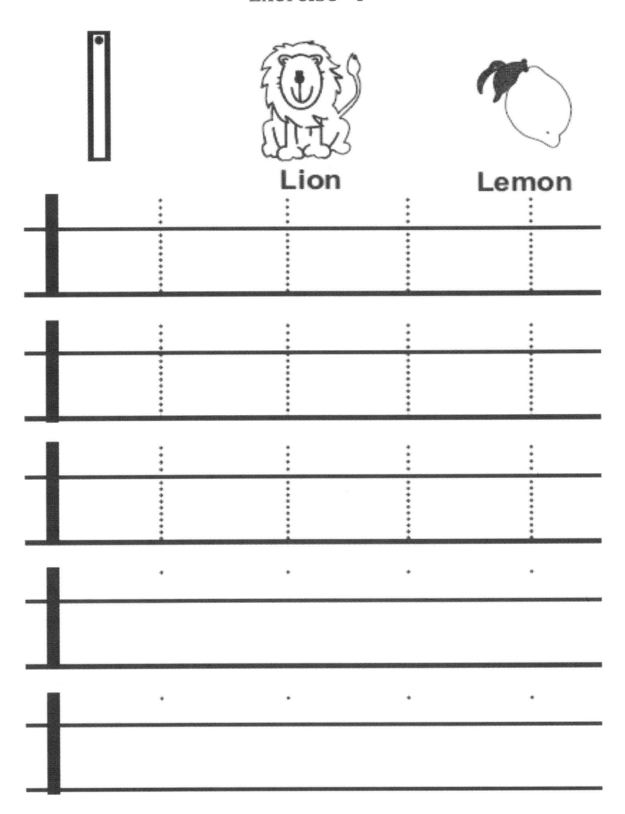

Lion

Lemon

Exercise - m

Monkey　　　**Moon**

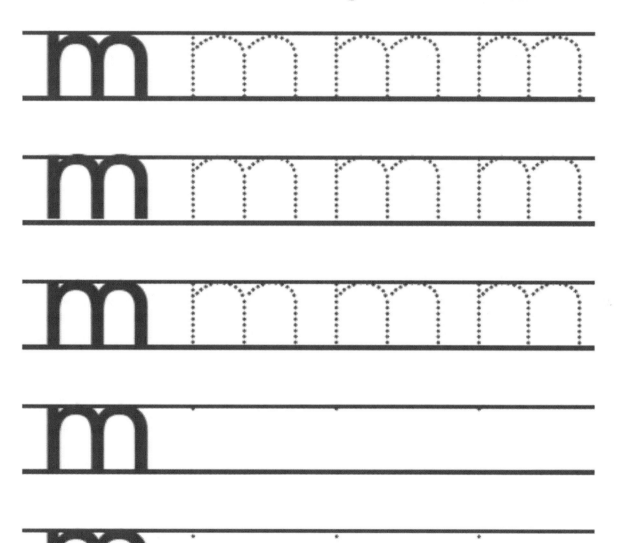

Exercise - n

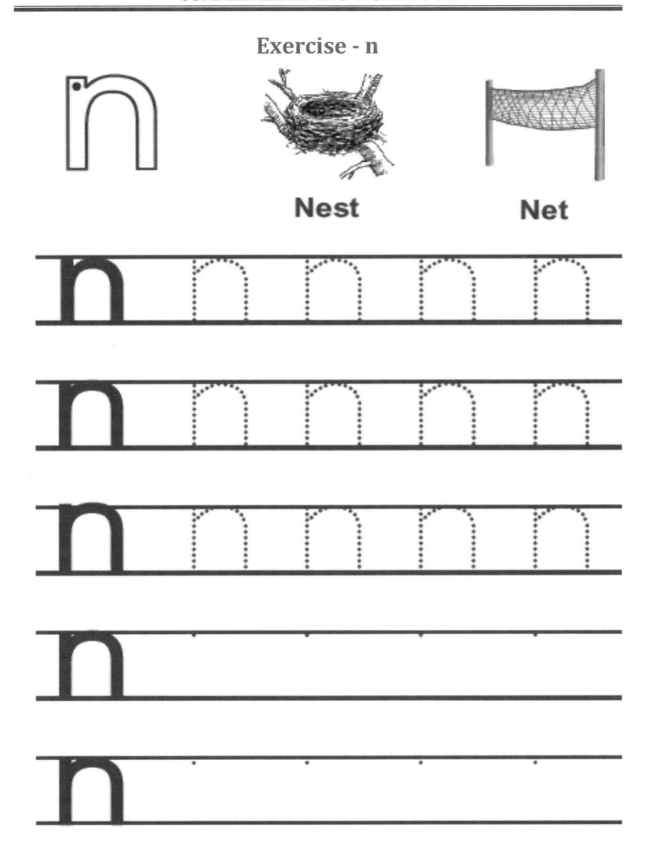

Nest **Net**

Exercise - o

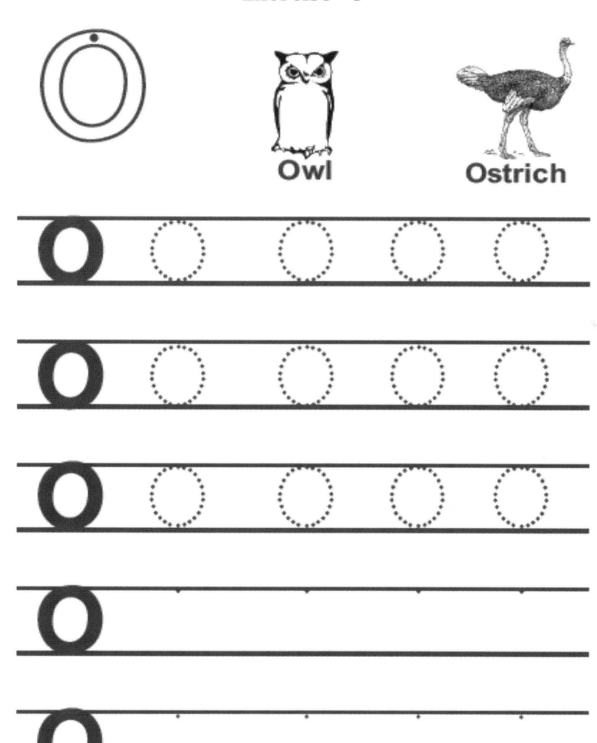

Owl

Ostrich

Exercise - p

Pig

Penguin

Exercise - q

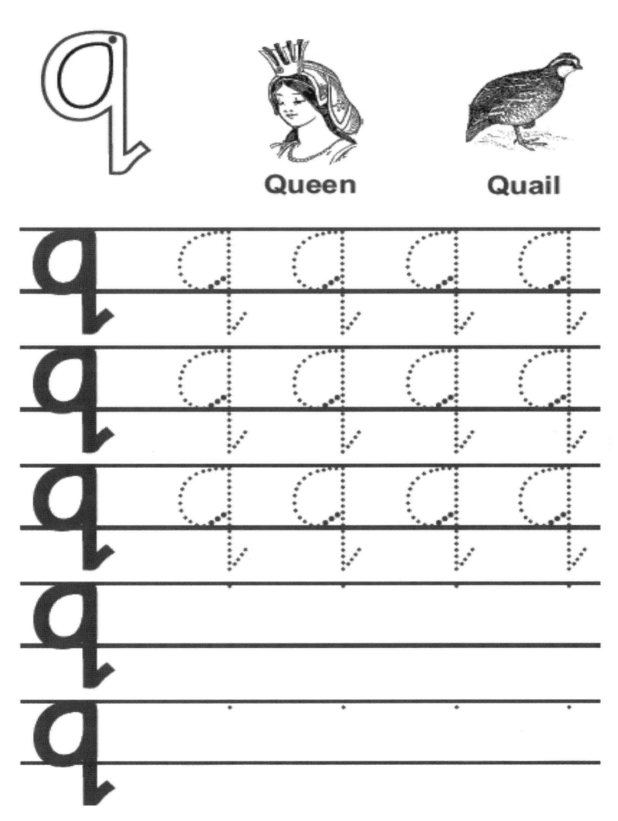

Queen

Quail

Exercise - r

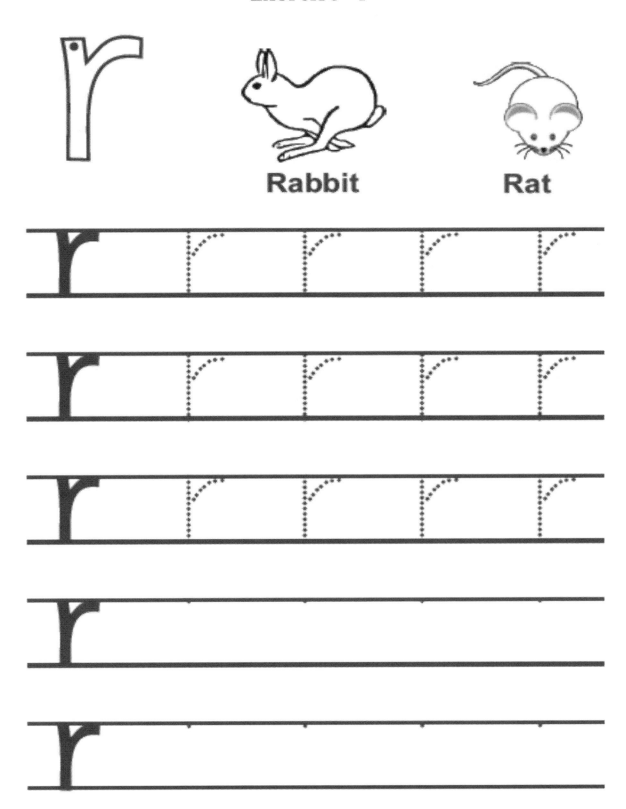

Rabbit   **Rat**

Exercise - s

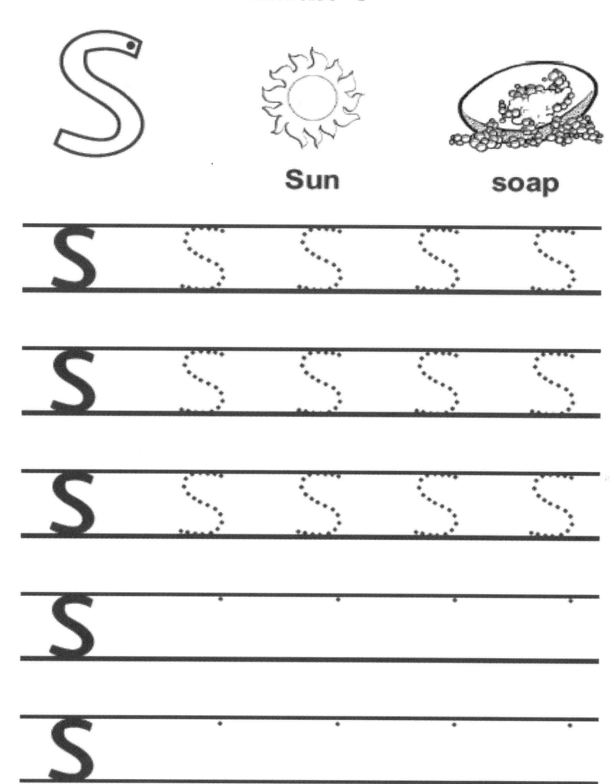

Sun   **soap**

SUMMER LEARNING WORKBOOK

Exercise - t

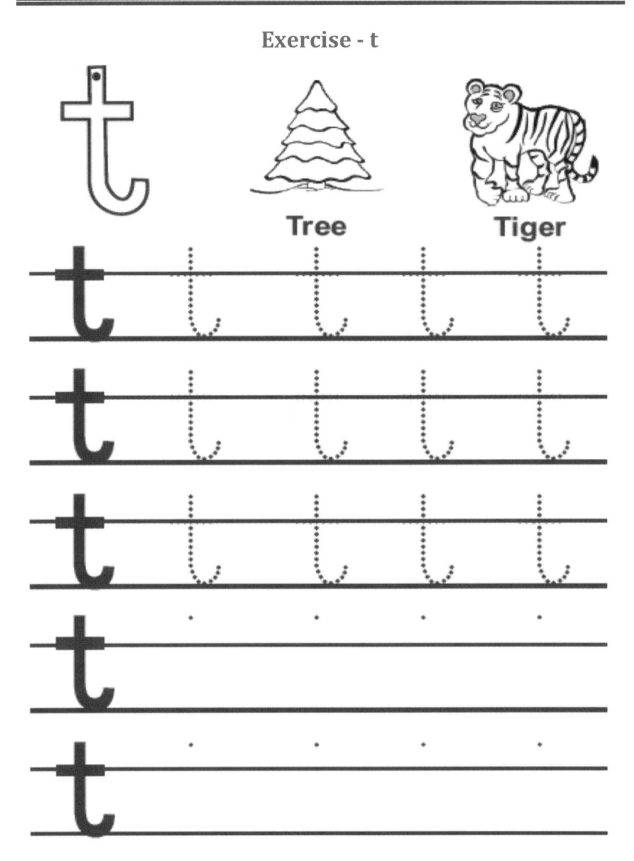

Tree

Tiger

Exercise - u

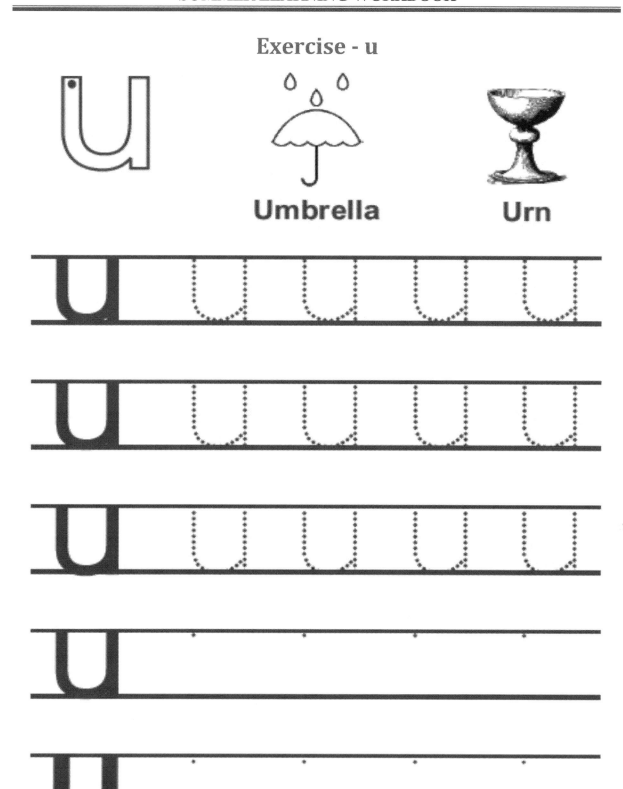

Umbrella **Urn**

Exercise - v

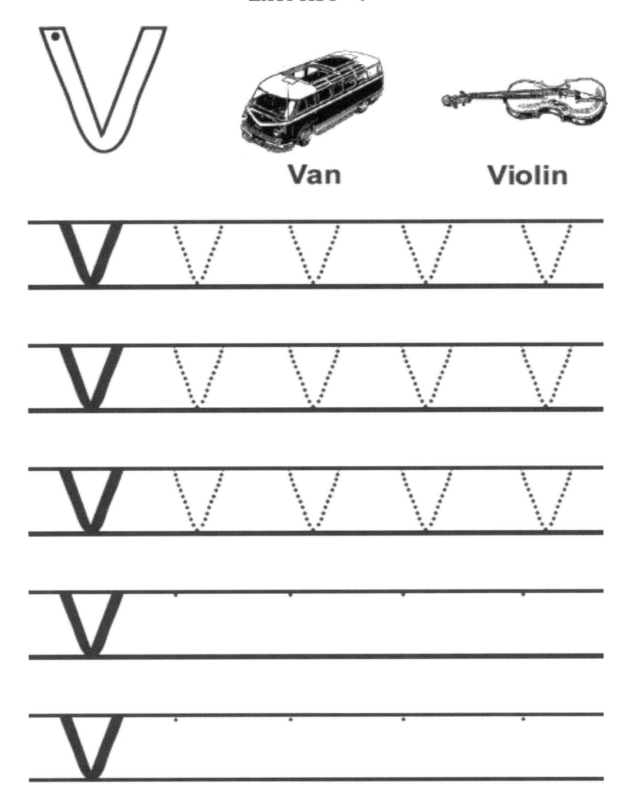

Van

Violin

Exercise - w

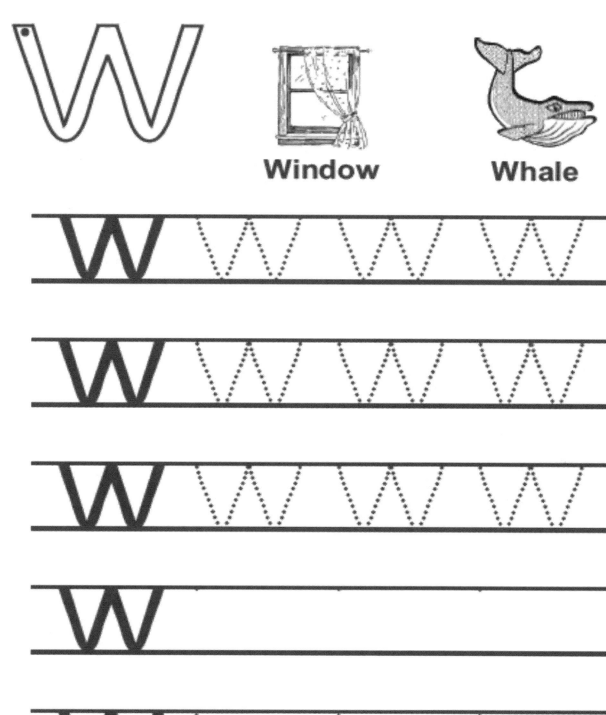

Window   **Whale**

Exercise – x

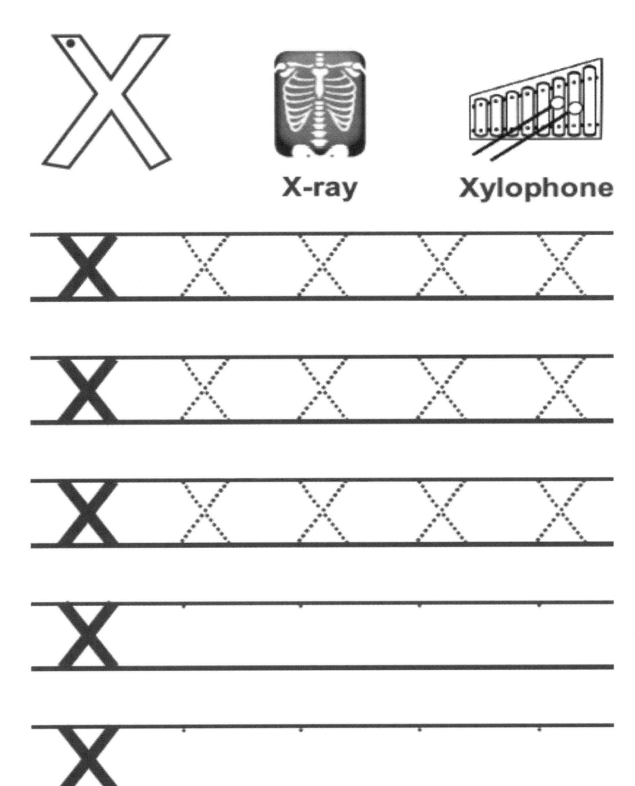

X-ray   Xylophone

Exercise - y

Yak

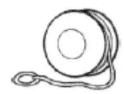

Yoyo

Exercise - z

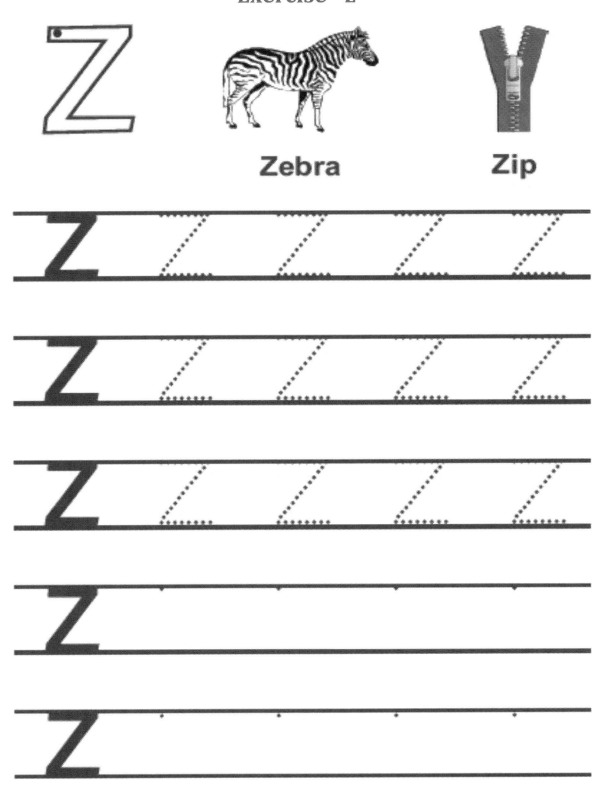

Zebra

Zip

More practice for Alphabets

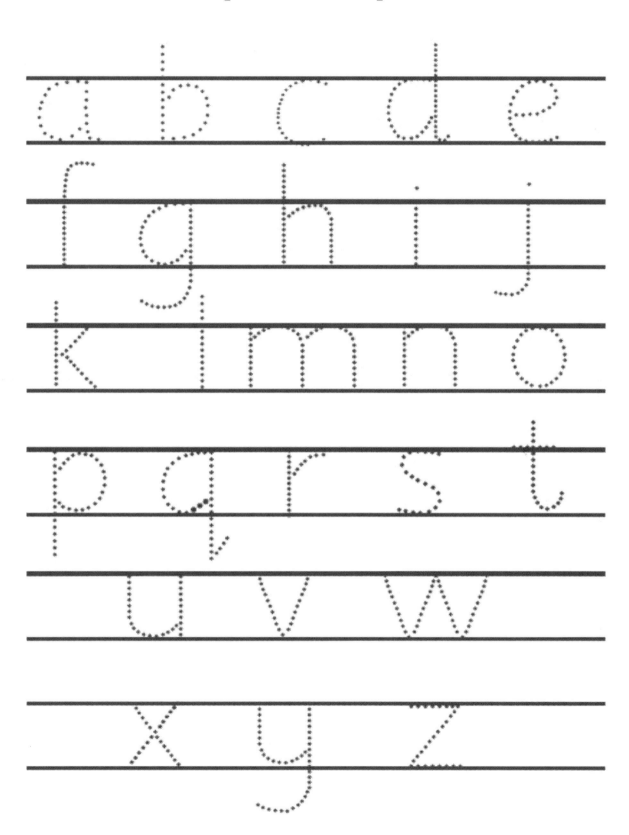

Dictation

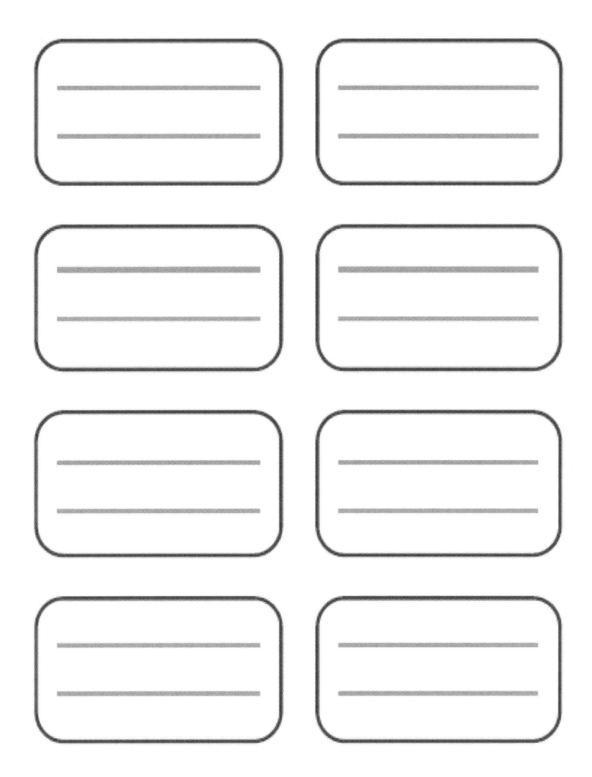

How can we keep ourselves clean?

Read 'Word Bank' carefully and write them on correct place.

Word Bank
Brushing Teeth
Combing Hair
Cutting Nails
Taking Bath
Washing Hands

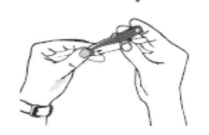

Circle the vowel letters

a   b   c   d

e   f   g   h

i   j   k   l

m   n   o   p

q   r   s   t

u   v   w   x

y   z

Write the beginning and ending letter of each picture.

Color the flowers and write the name of the color

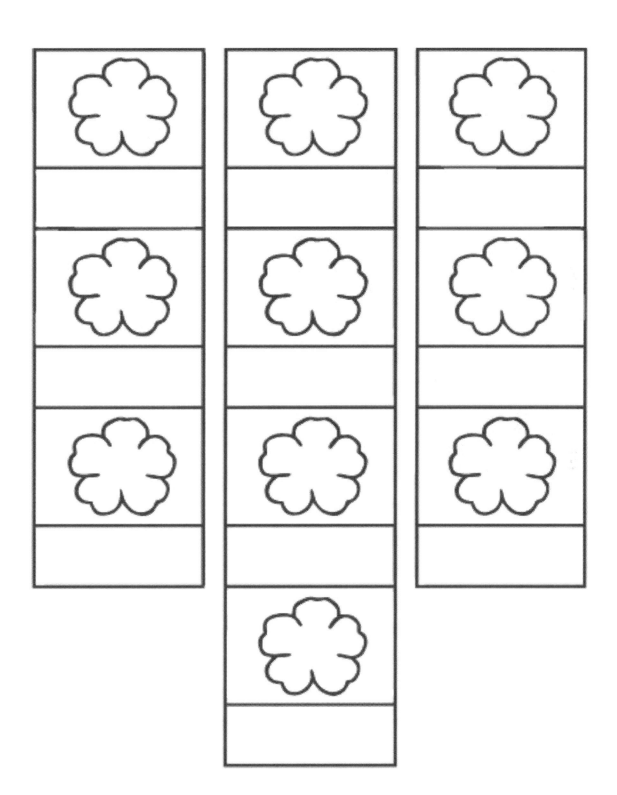

Days of the week

Remember the days of the week and write it at the end.

Monday	Tuesday
Wednesday	Thursday
Friday	Saturday

Sunday

Parts of the body

See the picture and write the parts of body.

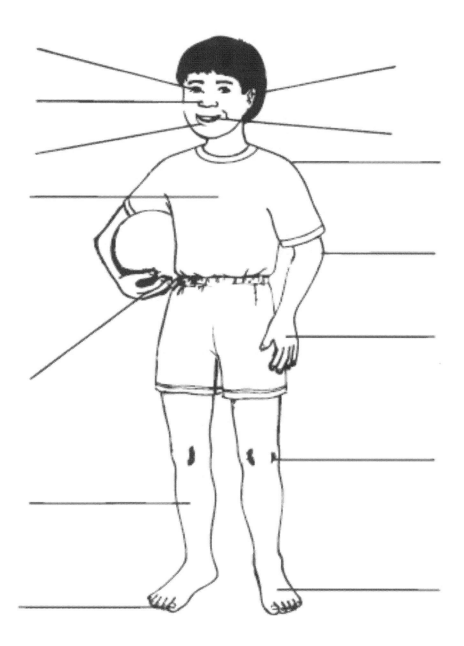

Fruits Names

See the picture and write the fruit name.

_____

_____

_____

_____

_____

Vegetables Names

See the picture and write the vegetable name.

_____

_____

_____

_____

_____

Names of Pet Animals

See the picture and write the name of the pet animal.

Names of shapes

See the picture and write the name of each shape.

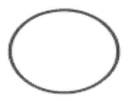

_____

_____

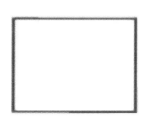

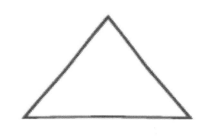

_____

_____

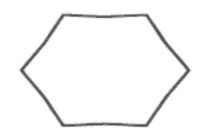

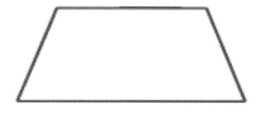

_____

_____

Word Bank

See the picture and fill in the blanks with the help of given words in Word Bank.

W
O
R   Kicking, Playing
          Reading, Flying
D   Swimming
Bank

Boy is ----------------- his ball.

Mother is -------------a book.

Girl is ----------------- with her doll.

The birds are --------------------------.

The ducks are --------------------------.

Missing Numbers

Write the missing numbers from 0 to 50.

Write the missing numbers from 51 to 100.

 **100**

Backward Counting

Write numbers counting backward from 20 to 0

Write numbers counting backward from 50 to 0

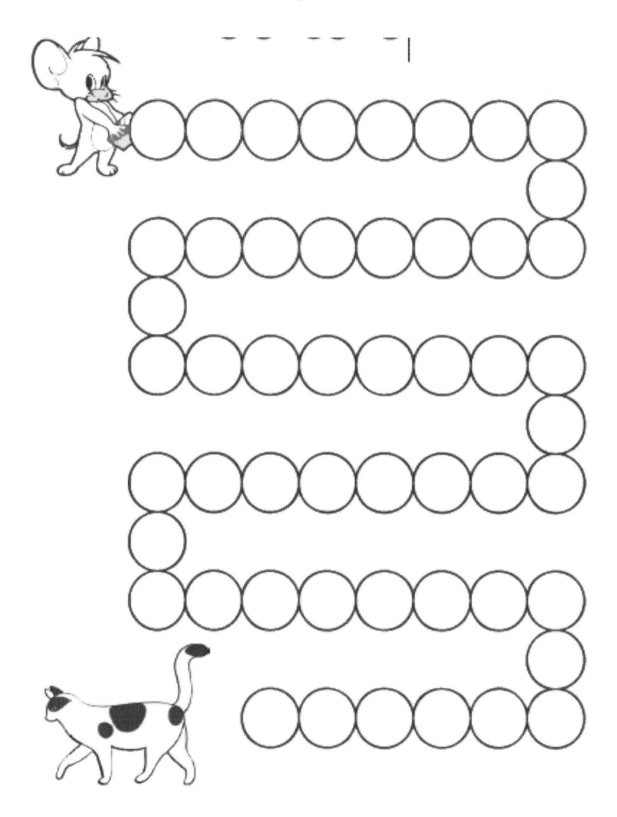

Color Counting

Count the colors and tick the correct answer

10   15   12   18   14   9

19   15   13   14   11   17

Dodges

Tick (✓) the smallest number in each box.

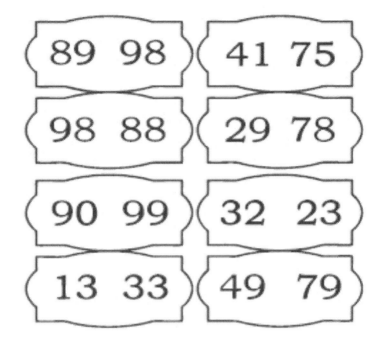

Circle the greater number.

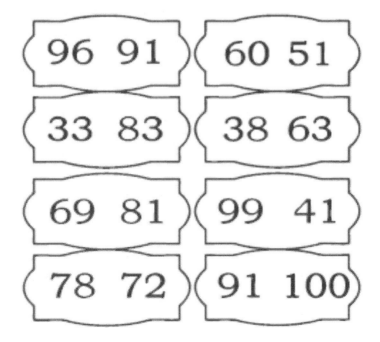

Numbers that comes before, after and between

Write the numbers that comes before, after and between

Before		After		Between	
....	18	11	....	12	 14
....	15	14	....	10	 12
....	9	17	....	0	 2
....	19	19	....	19	 17
....	12	0	....	16	 14
....	16	12	....	3	 1
....	13	8	....	13	 11
....	20	10	....	20	 18

Addition

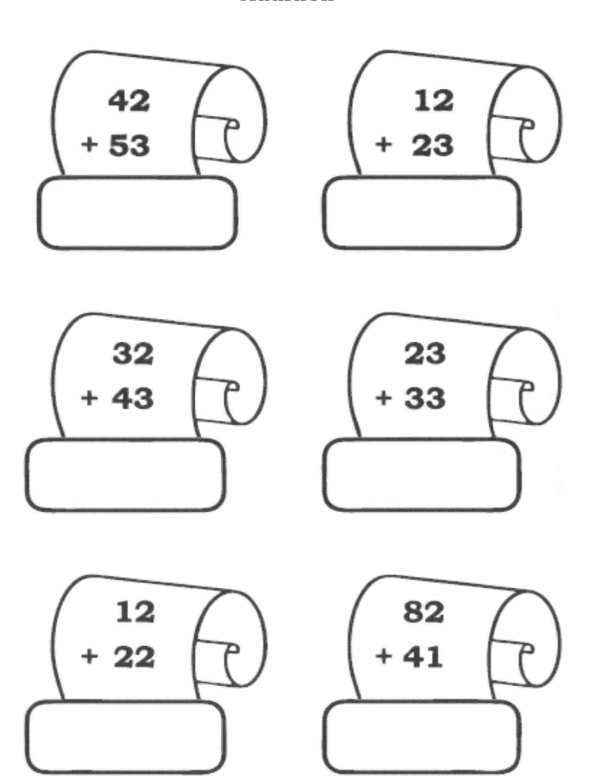

42
+ 53

12
+ 23

32
+ 43

23
+ 33

12
+ 22

82
+ 41

Count the numbers in the boxes, using the Abacus

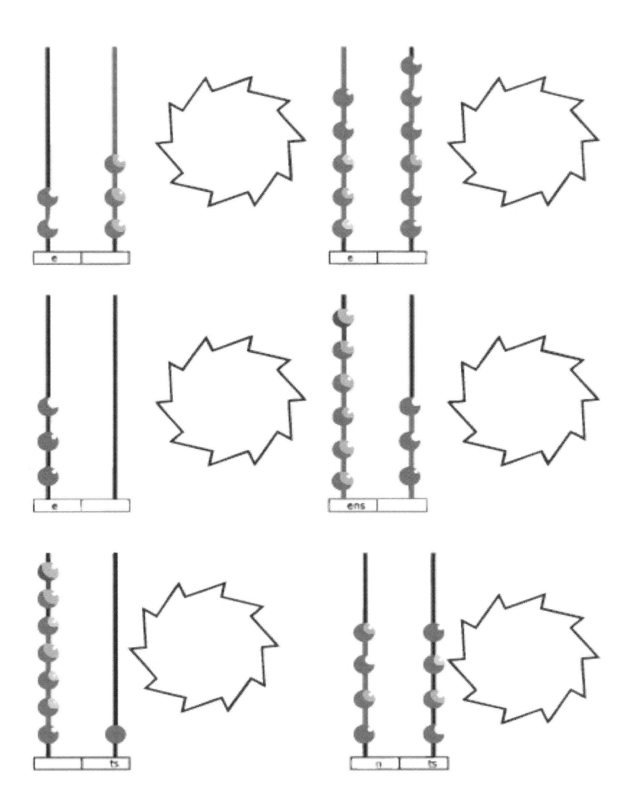

Subtraction

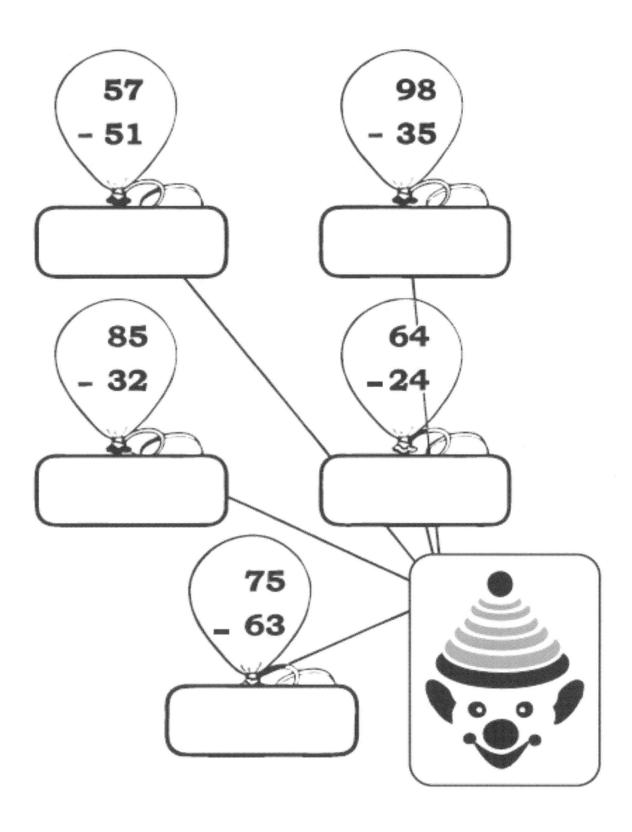

Multiplication

8
× 3

4
× 2

3
× 5

9
× 4

7
× 4

Division

$5 \overline{) 15}$ $2 \overline{) 18}$

$3 \overline{) 24}$ $5 \overline{) 45}$

$4 \overline{) 28}$

Table of "2"

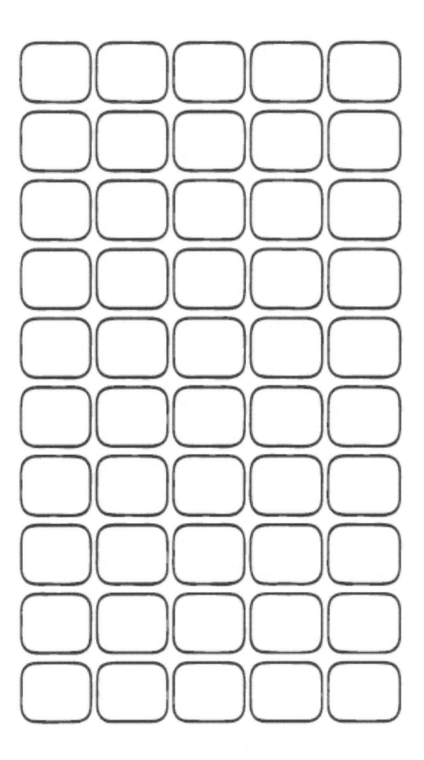

Table of "3"

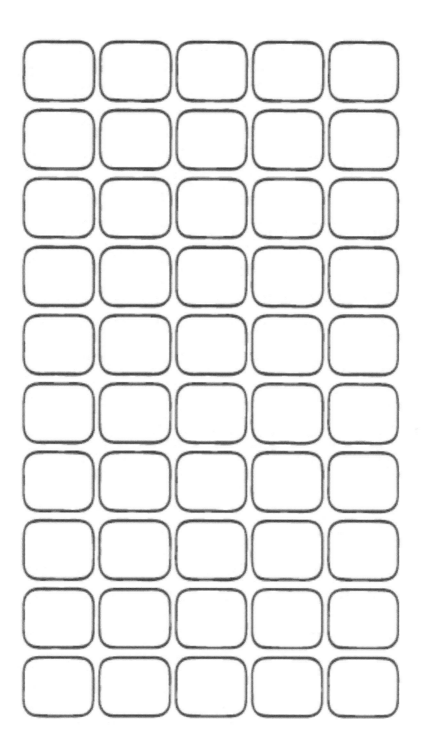

Table of "4"

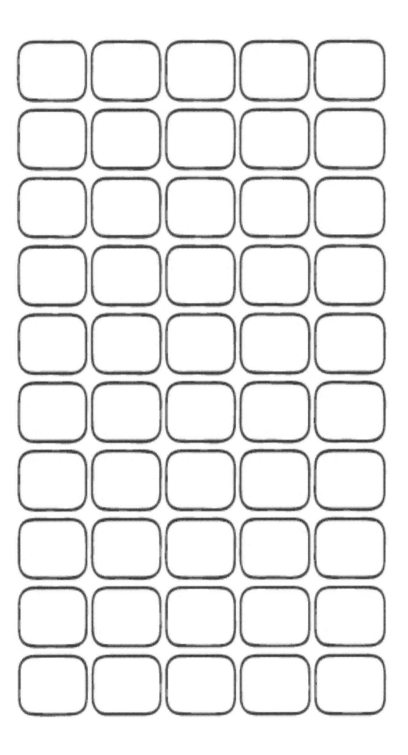

Table of "5"

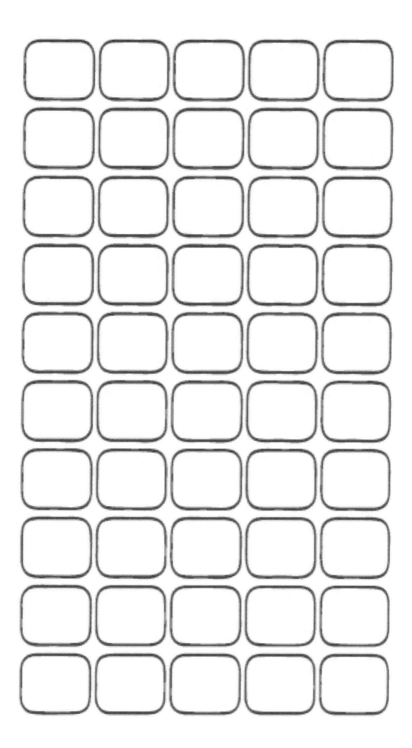

Table of "6"

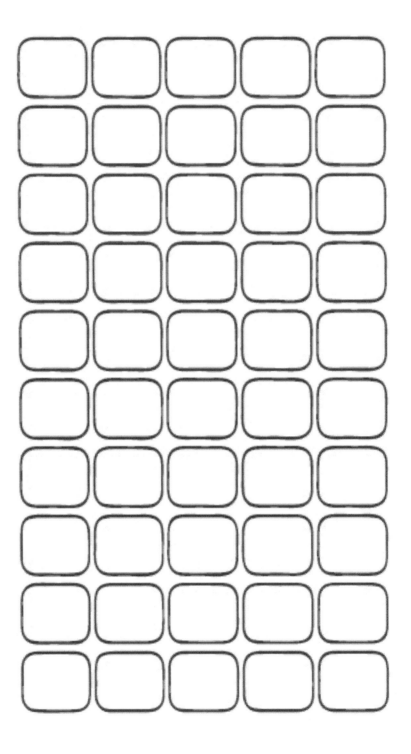

GOODBYE

Printed in Poland
by Amazon Fulfillment
Poland Sp. z o.o., Wrocław

55589224R00040